Pond-erings

Richard A. Budden

Copyright 2018 © Richard A. Budden

-The Lord Is My Shepherd-

When this life's fainting light
Ebbs away into night
And my sojourn on earth's at an end,
I've no dread of the grave,
From its power I'm saved,
For the Lord is my Shepherd and Friend

There's no want and no fear
For my Shepherd is near
And He leads me in pastures of green;
How my soul is restored
As I follow my Lord
By still waters of some quiet stream.

My steps are led right
Through the evening's twilight
In this valley where shadows grow long;
But no evil I dread in this land of the dead,
For to God doth my spirit belong.

Thy staff and thy rod are my fortress, O God,
Bringing comfort and strength to my soul;
My spirit is fed on thy bountiful bread.
And my cup of delight overflows.

Soon the trumpet will sound
And at last I'll be found
In a heaven that never will cease
In thy house I shall dwell
And all will be well
In thy kingdom of goodness and peace!

-You Sure Gave It To Them-

A sinner strode into the church one sunny, Sabbath day;
The preacher hoped that he could make him seek the Master's way,
And so he preached with sob and shout until the whole church shook;
But when the dust had settled and the preacher took a look,
The sinner rose quite unperturbed and with a sleepy grin
Addressed the preacher with these words: "you sure gave it to them."

Sunday after Sunday to the church the sinner came;
And when the service ended, the sinner said the same;
He pumped the preacher's hand with glee and added his amen
With words that rang from pew to pew, "you sure gave it to them."

And then a storm one Sabbath morn with blinding, drifting snow
Attacked the church with biting winds and piercing winter cold.
The preacher knew his people well and thought no one would dare
Attend the church on such a day but found the sinner there.

At last, the preacher said within, he's the only one who's here;
The sinner now will surely know these words are his to hear
And so the preacher preached his best on evil, sin, and hell
So hot the snow melt off the roof and 'round the church as well;

And when the preacher finished, said the sinner on his way,
Too bad they couldn't make it, you sure gave it to them today
The moral of this story is as plain as apple pie
Don't say "them" unto your preacher when all the time it's I!

-A Man He Was!-

A man he was
Of farms and such;
His hours were long
And his pay not much.

His life was simple:
His needs were few
And though his life
On earth is through.

The days God lent
Were blest to live
And were some of the best
The Lord could give.

Yes, he loved the land
And nature's sounds
And the joys he prized
In his home were found.

His country life
Was quite enough,
For he had no need
Of that other stuff

That other folks all
Seemed to crave
And hungrily sought
From cradle to grave.

For the more these others
On earth did gain,
The more they wanted
And the more they complained.

Just a modest man,
But that t'weren't bad;
For he held far more
Than some others had!

A faithful wife
Whom he loved so dear,
Who shared his life
Year after year.

And children whom
He was pleased to raise,
A special blessing
All his days.
Aye, a man he was
So good and kind,
A loyal friend.
That is hard to find.

A country man
Until the day he died;
Now he lives anew
On the other side

With the Lord he served
Until his days were done;
Now he hears Christ say,
"My son, well done!"

-Only 80-

Dear Lord, I'm only 80,
And there's much I haven't done;
So would you let me live at least
Until I'm 81?

Then if I haven't finished all
That I would like to do,
Please, may I stay here longer
Until I'm 82?

So many places I would go;
So much I'd like to see
Could I have your approval
To live on to 83?

Yes, there's so much on earth to do,
So much that's still in store;
And so I ask may I remain
Until I'm 84?

And if I'm still around by then
And find myself alive,
You might as will just leave me here
Until I'm 85!

So fast the world is changing
That I'd really like to stick
Around and see what happens If I live to 86.

I know it must be nice up there
To live with You in Heaven;
But if it's all the same to You
Please grant me 87.

I know by then I won't be fast,
And sometimes I'll be late;
Yet it would be so pleasant if
I reached age 88.

Long life on earth you've given me
I've had a glorious time.
So if it's not too much to ask
Let me reach 89.

Dear Lord, I'm really on a roll;
I'm old and getting fat.
So just give me what you think best,
And I'll be glad with that!!!

-Little Grapes Are Growing-

In the vineyard of our God
Little grapes are growing
As they soak up sun and rain
In their hearts they're knowing
That within they have the power
To be weak or brazen
And become the finest wine
Or just a shriveled raisin.

In the likeness of the grape,
We too are preparing
For the shriveling of self
Or a life of sharing.
Soon will come our harvest time;
And on that occasion,
Will we be the finest wine
Or just a shriveled raisin?!

-The Needle & Thread Prayer-

Dear God, who art in heaven,
I make this vow to you,
No matter what you ask of me
I will be quick to do.

Dear Lord, you be the needle,
And I will be the thread;
Just go before me where you will,
And there I will be led.

For where you lead, I'll follow
And do the best I can
To glorify your holy name
And bless my fellowman.

Please lead on, Holy Spirit,
Sew by your grace within
A new world stitched with threads of love.
In Jesus' name. Amen!

-A Graduate's Prayer-

A task has been completed
And a goal has been attained;
Through work and perseverance
Tools of learning we have gained

An episode in school days
Has been written, now is o'er
And we stand upon the threshold
Of our future's open door.

We know not what awaits us
In tomorrow's great unknown;
But we enter it with courage,
For we do not go alone

Walk beside us, gracious Father,
Grant us strength and will to do
What would make our lives a blessing
To the world, ourselves, and you.

Help us live our days in service
So that at life's setting sun,
We may graduate with honors
And hear your words, "Well done!"

-Freedom-

Hear the call of freedom;
Take it to your hearts.
It's among the greatest gifts
Our gracious God imparts.

Heed the voice of freedom;
Obey it now this hour.
For freedom without action
Is stripped of all its power.

Freedom is not passive
To store away in vault;
Use its treasure wisely,
Or lose it by default.

Freedom is like gold dust
Within our mortal hand;
It slips through careless fingers
Like grains of flowing sand.

For foolish is as foolish does
When selfishness within
Has driven freedom from our souls
And made us slaves of sin.

Freedom is not natural
To the carnal man;
He wastes it soon on trifles,
And sees it not again.

Yes, freedom's for the children
Of the Lord above;
Freedom only comes through Christ

Who fills us with His love!

Freedom's only wasted
On a selfish soul,
For freedom's only kept alive
By godly self-control.

Freedom is like daylight
That greets us as the dawn
We tend to have it for awhile.
And then it soon is gone.

Freedom's not a license
To flitter on some whim,
But freedom used responsibly
Can then be born again.

Yes, if we use our freedom
For good and not for ill,
Then it remains alive in us,
And it always will.

But know that if we turn from God
And choose instead our sin,
Then freedom's force will ebb away
And never come again!

-The Old Switch-A-Roo-

Have a pity party;
Jacob was deceived!
'Neath that pretty bridal veil,
Rachel he perceived.

Truly was he so in love
One girl filled his mind;
What a rude awakening
Another one to find!

For, alas, some villain
Pulled the bait and switch;
Yes, there were two sisters,
But Jacob knew not which

One lay down beside him
On his wedding bed.
He thought he'd married Rachel
But got Leah there instead!

Yes, he expected Rachel;
What a big surprise.
When he wasn't looking,
Someone changed the brides!

Let this be a lesson, guys;
Check a time or two
Lest you be the victim
Of the old switch-a-roo!

-The Sound of Angel Wings-

Of all of God's most treasured things,
The best of all is angel wings
Their sound is music to our ear,
Reminding us our Lord is near.

And when He wants to share His love,
God sends an angel from above;
And by His power a child is born
An angel clothed in human form.

This little blessing that we know
Within our hearts will live and grow;
And with each utterance she sings.
The lovely song of angel wings,

Now on this very special day,
We offer her to God and pray
Our thanks for all the joy she bring
And for the sound of angel wings!

-Kyrsten-

We are gathered here
In this sacred place
To savor a measure
Of God's sweet grace.

A touch of Heaven
In our mortal midst
That exceeds by far
All we hoped or wished.

Remember that day
When she came to us
And placed in our keeping
Her treasured trust?

Remember how God
From the great unknown
Put her little hand
Into our own,

And bade us bathe
Her in our love
To blend our own
With His above?

Yes, we remember
Those big blue eyes
That gazed at us
Through azure skies.

And she grants to us
As only she can
The warmth of her smile
And the touch of her hand.

Yes, with grateful hearts
We now dedicate
A body so small
But a spirit so great.

To the Lord to whom
She really belongs
Who fills our souls
With joyful songs.

And we promise this day
That we always will give
What Kyrsten needs
To laugh and to live.

All praise to God
In this sacred place
For this wondrous gift
Of His love and grace!

-Second Fiddle-

Instruments made for music;
What's the hardest one to play?
Though that's difficult to answer,
This is what the sages say:

Yes, the answer that is wisest
To this poignant, little riddle
Is the one that is the hardest
Surely is the second fiddle!

All the world is filled with people
Who would play first violin
But if all would play that music,
it would really be a sin.

Melody, or course, is needed;
But how dull that it would be
If there were no second fiddles
To provide the harmony

So it is with us as Christians:
Christ must truly play the lead,
And the part of second fiddle
He bestows on you and me.

Beautiful is second fiddle
If we'll die to selfish pride;
Only then within our spirits
Can God's music there abide

Yes, the strains of Heaven's music
Only are so rich and sweet
Cause we play the second fiddle,
And the music is complete!

-A Love Prayer-

I love you, precious Jesus,
For everything you are;
Yes, you exceed all other loves
Within my heart by far.

I love you for your mercy;
For though you know my sin,
With grace you have forgiven me
In spite of what I've been

I love you, gracious Saviour,
For having faith in me
When others doubt what I can do
And what my life can be.

I love you for the patience
That you have deep within
Which reassures me when I fail
That I should try again.

I love you, blessed Jesus,
For all these things and more,
But there is something special
That I adore you for.

Yes, I not only love you
For all that you may be,
But also for the gift of love
When you created me.
For anything of value
That I may be or do
In this world or the one to come
I owe, my Lord, to you!

-Bothered?-

The Devil seldom bothers me,
The sinful soul may say,
But Satan needs not trouble those
That he owns anyway.

No man can see how much enslaved
He is until he's stood
Against the Devil and his ways
And tried to do the good.

For Satan, like a fisherman
Knows it would be for nought
To cast his line into the pail
Of fish already caught

-Fishing's More Than Wishing-

Just sitting still and wanting fish
Will make no angler great;
The Lord may send the fish to us,
But we must dig the bait.

It may seem nice to us, my friends,
As on the lake we float,
If we could nap and have the fish
Just jump into our boat!

But God has put us on this pond
To do far more than snore;
For as we sleep our lives away
What does He need us for?

Yes, we are called to fish for souls,
And that means more than wishing;
So let's get busy while we may
And really do some fishing!

-Never Too Busy!-

Never too busy to feed a soul
Who needs my help to reach his goal;
Never too busy to take the time
To help someone in his upward climb.

Never too busy to stop my task
Whenever a needy person should ask;
Never too busy to listen awhile,
To wipe a tear, or to share a smile.

Never too busy to feed God's lamb
And nourish his life however I can;
Never to busy my love to impart;
Never too busy to give him my heart.

Never too busy to lighten his load
Whether that person be young or old;
Never too busy to heed his call
Regardless if he's great or small.

Never too busy for someone to pray
No matter how full my schedule today
Never too busy to lead him to Christ
Whatever else I sacrifice.

Never too busy to lift him from sin
Though he should fall again and again;
Never too busy to help with a smile
And walk with him that second mile.

Never too busy while on this earth
To help another enhance his worth;
Never too busy will I ever be
For God's never been too busy for me!

-Smile-

A smile's such a little thing
To share along life's way,
But it can warm a person's heart
And brighten up his day.

It doesn't cost a single cent
To give someone a smile,
And it can be just what he needs
To make his life worthwhile.

Though it seems strange, there is a truth
By which this world is guided;
That joy is always multiplied
Whenever it's divided.

So if you have the joy of God,
Don't keep it locked within;
But let it out with friendly smiles
Or with a great, big grin.

Just let the corners of your mouth
Be raised to God in prayer;
And when the joy flows from your soul,
A smile will be there.

Yes, give a smile away today
To everyone you meet;
And when you do, you will receive
A very special treat.

For you will find a smile's more
Contagious than the flu;
And when you smile at others, soon
They're smiling back at you.

-Questions-

Small children weep while parents fight,
And addicts curse their wretched plight;
A victim's lowered 'neath the sod
And we exclaim, "Oh, where is God?"

Our nation crumbles from within
As folks are hated for their skin;
No longer are race riots odd;
And we keep asking, "Where is God?"

We take a husband or a wife,
But seldom take we one for life;
The bitter fruits of going mod
Cause us to cry out, "Where is God?"

A graveside family in despair,
There is no hope to help it there;
All life seems like an empty pod;
And we are wondering, "Where is God?"

Through bone and flesh cruel missiles tear;
The horrors of war are everywhere;
And in the chaos we still prod
With the same question, "Where is God?"

We ponder if God could be dead,
Or if He might be lost instead;
But, oh, if we could only see
The dead and lost are you and me.

It is not God who went away,
But rather we who've gone astray;
And now He looks for me and you
So He may give us life anew.

The Lord, as in fair Eden's land,
Knows all about the deeds of man;
To save us from the sins we do
Our God is calling, "Where are you?"

On Sunday mornings, bright and fair,
He looks in church to see who's there;
And when He sees our empty pew
The Lord keeps asking, "Where are you?"

Yes, "Where is God?" we often say;
But the big question for today
As taken from God's point for view
Is simply this, friend, "Where are you?"

-Such Simple Things-

We need to be reminded of
The life that Jesus led
O that our souls by thought of it
Can day by day be fed

It is so easy to forget
What Jesus did one day,
For things of this world fill our minds
And his deed slips away.

But then we drink the fruit of grapes
And taste the bread of grain;
Such simple things, but they recall
What we need to retain.

For as we share these elements,
They kindle in the soul
The memories of what Christ did
So many years ago

T'was at his final meal with friends
Before that fateful day,
When He would die upon a cross
To take our sins away,

That Jesus took a loaf to bread
And broke it lovingly And said,
"This is my body which
Is given unto thee."

Likewise He took a common cup
And gave to all to drink
So that whene'er they quenched their thirst,
Of him they'd pause to think.

That cup proclaimed salvation's means
Through what the Christ would do;
He blood would pour like flowing wine
So men could live anew.

Such simple things are food and drink,
And yet they help us see
What Christ in love would do upon
A cross for you and me.

-Sleep-

Our sleep is such a pleasant thing,
A boon to all mankind;
For by it we are all renewed
In body and in mind.

How sweet a tender baby's sleep
Upon his mother's breast;
How good the slumber of a man
Who from his labor rests,

So blessed is a patient's sleep
Whose body suffers pain;
So welcomed to a fearful child
Who longs for dawn again.

Yes, precious is this gift of God
Who gave it for our sake;
Yet we're created not to sleep
But made to be awake!

We're fashioned in the likeness
Of the God who does not sleep
But watches over us in love
Our souls from sin to keep.

And though our bodies may need rest
Our spirits need to be
Awake and serving Christ the Lord
In this world constantly

For there are many souls to save
And battles to be won;
But if we sleep this life away,
These tasks will not get done.
So let us stay awake, my friends,
For we cannot afford
To fall asleep within the Church
And disappoint our Lord.

Church sleeping can be dangerous
For every man of dust
Because such slumber well could be
The sleep of death for us!

-Pity The Poor Atheist!-

Pity the poor atheist!
A man too often with degrees
In human wisdom's lore
Which lead him to the third degree
That Jesus has in store.

Pity the poor atheist!
A man whose head feels twice its size
Whose spirit has turned sour
But won't admit that he is drunk
On too much worldly power.

Pity the poor atheist!
A man whose choice possession is
An unbeliever's laugh
But it's poor compensation for
A just Creator's wrath.

Pity the poor atheist!
A man in night whose only aid
A whistle to keep strong,
He longs to pray but just can't say
Perhaps he has been wrong.

Pity the poor atheist!
A man whose disillusioned soul
Knows not how to behave,
For no one is an atheist
One step beyond the grave!

Pity the poor atheist!

-The Still and the Storm-

Be not afraid of the storms of life
No matter how fierce the wind;
For the Lord stilled the storms of Galilee
And He surely can do it again

But it isn't always the will of God
To still the angry sea,
For He knows there are times to let storms rage
When it's best for you and me.

If God for us calms every storm
And from every gale He saves
Then there never would be a tumultuous sea
For us to walk on its waves.

How sad it would be for God's children to miss
The full extent of his plan,
For on the waves of the mightiest seas
He increases the faith of man.

Yes, faith is the fount of a thousand gifts,
The birth of a million dreams
And walking the Sea of our Galilee
Is not as hard as it seems.

For the Lord gives faith to those who ask
Yes, it's part of His will for us.
The key to success is the choice we make
As to where we place our trust.

So just accept the storms when the come
Rejoice when the waves grow high
And Christ we'll see in the lightning's flash
Silhouetted against the sky.

When He bids us come to walk to Him,
Then our faith can be reborn;
And it will grow until its strength
Will far exceed the storm.
So let us keep our eyes on Christ
And never mind the gale;
For Jesus takes us by the hand,
And He will never fail.

Yes, there are times God calms the storm
When the wind blows fierce and wild,
But other times He stills the storm,
And instead He calms His child!

-It Isn't Easy Being a Nail-

It isn't easy being a nail;
Yes, that is very true.
Imagine spending all your life
With someone pounding on you.

But being a nail is a special job,
And I tell you from my heart
That without nails the things we need
Would simply fall apart.

Just think if nails would go on strike,
Then where would we all be
With houses, schools, and churches too
Crashing on you and me?

But it isn't easy being a nail
And getting hit on your head;
Yes, how much better it would feel
To be the hammer instead!

Yet Jesus chose to be a nail
Because He saw that we
Had fallen apart because of our sins
And were nothing more than debris

So Jesus came to be our nail
That was driven into a cross
To die for our sins so you and I
Would not be forever lost.

Yes, it isn't easy being a nail;
But Jesus came from above
To be the nail that holds us firm
To our heavenly Father in love

Oh, it isn't easy being a nail
But won't you be one too?
So that the power and love of Christ
Can strengthen others through you!

-The Lamp Lighter-

The streets of the earth
Were engulfed by the night,
And men in their darkness
Had lost their sight.

They stumbled and fell
As they groped all about
In the blackness of sin
And the midnight of doubt.

Then into the world
The Lamp Lighter came
To dispel all the night
By the light of His flame.

As He kindles with fire
The lanterns of men,
There is light where before
Only darkness had been!

As the Lamp Lighter looks
Into our hearts tonight,
Are we part of the darkness
Or part of the light?

-So Many Trees-

So many trees God grants to us
Reflecting human traits;
What do they whisper to our souls
Of our immortal fates?

The Oak seems such a glorious tree
But really is a shrew
That won't give up its old leaves
'Til forced to by the new!

Then there's the Silver Maple tree,
The litterest bug around;
It scatters all its trashy leaves
And branches on the ground.

And there's the Crab that in the spring
Fair flowers flaunting show,
But it's among the first to fade
When winter breezes blow!

And last, behold the Fraser Fir,
The grandest tree I've seen;
It speaks of everlasting life
With needles soft and green!

So many trees God grants to us,
And in them we can trust
To see the clues He places there
Of how He looks on us!

-Do Yourself A Flavor!-

I'm your little teapot,
Come, and you will see;
Do yourself a flavor;
Fall in love with me!

I'll be your companion,
Steeped to suit your taste,
Adding to your pleasure
Rather than your waist!

Revel in my friendship,
Bathe now in my brew.
I'll be your sustainer;
I will pamper you!

Try my dainty tea cups.
Coffee mugs are crude;
Cups enhance the flavor
Of your favorite food.

Yes, draw near and savor
Heaven's recipe:
Honest tea is always
The best policy!

I'm your little buddy,
Short and rather stout;
Come, and turn me over;
You'll love what comes out!

-The Less Or The Best-

Why is it, my friends,
That we settle for less
When God in His bounty
Would give us His best?

Yes, why do we toil
For things of this earth
And ignore Heaven's treasures
Of far greater worth?

So now like the Prodigal
Son in Christ's tale.
Let us come to ourselves,
And refusing to fail!

Yes, our Father is calling;
Let's run unto Him,
Forsaking our pride
And repenting our sin!

We'll find Him awaiting
With arms open wide;
Let's walk through the Door
And we'll find Him inside!

Let's give up the Mammon;
Embrace God instead.
In His house we'll be happy
Our souls be well-fed!

Let's not hesitate;
For the sake of our soul
Come, let the Lord touch us;
And He'll make us whole!

Yes, let us not settle
For that which is less,
For God waits in Heaven
To give us His best!

-Be Faithful!-

The Devil played Adam and Eve for a fool
In the Garden of Eden one day;
Their pride was too great for them to resist,
So the Lord they failed to obey.

And as a result, the rest of their lives
They paid for their guilt and their blame;
And though the Lord may have granted them grace,
Their lives were never the same!

So be wise enough to learn here today
From the error of our kith and kin;
Let's choose to obey the sweet voice of God
And avoid all the pitfalls of sin.

May we opt on this day not only to choose
The forgiveness that comes from God's Son,
But also be faithful to His precious Name
'Til our journey on earth here is done.

Yes, it's never enough just to enter a race,
For it's only he who's so bold
That he will be faithful no matter the cost
Who's the winner and brings home the gold!

-Rover's Bach-

A trained dog entertained the guests,
The classics he did play
Upon a grand piano
In a most peculiar way.

A matron tried to pet the pooch
Which growled at her advance;
In terror she withdrew her hand,
Her safety to enhance.

The owner of the dog spoke up,
"There is no need for fright,
For I assure you Rover's Bach
Is far worst than his bite!"

-The Knight Of the Road-

Past the huge, regal factory
And the humble abode,
He pilots his rig:
He's the knight of the road!

Yes, in all kinds of weather
'Neath the stars and the sun,
He's horsepower driven
To finish his run.

His steeds in obedience
Do what they are told;
For he is their master,
The knight of the road.

Yes, for year after year
And for mile upon mile,
He challenged them all
With his grit and his smile.

Now at last he's completed
One last needful run
On the highway to Heaven
With Jesus the Son.

No longer this knight
Through the darkness must roam,
For he's finished his course
And he's found his way home.

So let us remember
The knight of the road
Who now drives his rig
On the highways of gold.

And remember the Lord
Who directed this knight,
For He'll also guide us
If we follow His light.

Yes, we're all on a journey,
And it's no pedal run;
So let us be faithful
To Jesus the Son!

-Give a Little Whistle-

Whistle past the graveyard;
Blow a little tune;
Make peace with the spirits
Lest it spell your doom!

Keep the ghosts there happy;
Show them you're their friend;
If you make them angry,
That could mean your end!

Will a cheerful whistle
Keep a ghost at bay?
I don't know the answer,
But try it anyway!

Yes, give a little whistle;
It could be a charm;
Though it may not do much good,
It can't do any harm!

-Only One-

Only one life is offered,
Only one chance to live,
Only one try per person
Doth our Creator give!

Where will you place your ante,
How will you bet your soul,
Will you select Christ Jesus
Or give the Devil control?

Yes, life on earth is fleeting;
Opt twixt the Saviour and sin.
Now is your time for choosing,
And it won't come again!

-A Labor Day Prayer-

Our Father God, in whom we trust
We know our prayers are heard;
We thank you for our life in Christ
And for the chance to serve

As willing workers for your Name
Until your Son shall come
Or 'til at last you call us home
And our work here be done.

We ask not for less work to do,
For many need our care;
We only ask for strength from you
So we can do our share.

Grant us compassion, gracious God,
For those whose souls we feed,
Especially for those so blind
They cannot see their need.

Impress upon our play-proned minds
Each day, we humble ask,
The overwhelming urgency
Of our appointed task

To win and nurture souls for you
Through Christ who came to give
His life upon a rugged cross
So all of us may live.

Our foes have tried to tempt our souls
With doubts and days of ease,
But you have taught us thorough your Son
How we should handle these.

Thus, like our Lord in faithfulness,
We'll work each day for you
And have no time to waste on earth
As others seem to do.

For we know if our work is slack
That great will be the cost
As human souls we should have won
Will be forever lost.

So 'til our sun sets, Father God,
Renew us from within,
And we shall work as one with Christ,
In Jesus' Name, Amen!

-A Bit More-

A bit more tired at the close of day,
A bit less push to have my own way,

A bit less ready to judge and blame,
A bit less seeking my foes to shame.

A bit more patience with noisy youth,
A bit more looking for the ultimate truth,

A bit more focused on others' views,
A bit more time for the Bible's Good News,

A lot more aiding what others can be,
A lot more of Christ and a lot less of me!

-A Rainbow of Memories-

A rainbow of memories
In glittering hue,
A basket of dreams
That remind us of you.

A handful of yesterdays
Eager to share,
All tied with a ribbon
In our hearts with care.

Your smile so radiant
Lit up our life-
Our mother, our friend,
Our granny, our wife.

The family God gave you
To nurture and raise
Now stands as a tribute
To your love and praise.

So rest from your labors
In blessed release;
You're safe now with Jesus
In His perfect peace.

Your pain now is over,
And each tear is dried.
Your soul has been tested,
Your faith has been tried.

And out of it all,
You've emerged by God's grace
To be with your Saviour
Who prepared you a place.

Yes, a rainbow of memories
Of you we hold dear;
What a wonderful privilege
Of knowing you here.

Yes, our glorious memories
Of you are so nice,
And the comfort they give
For now must suffice.

But we're looking to Heaven
When our time will come
To join you someday
By the side of the Son.

Then more than just memories
Our glad hearts will know,
For we'll all share up there
As we did here below.

And we'll all be together
By the grace of God's Son
Who will whisper of you,
"My child, well done!"

-A Poetry Puzzle-

It is a place we all have been,
But prob'ly never will again.

It is important to us all,
But not a place we can recall.

It is a place where dark's the norm,
Yet without light it's nice and warm.

It is a good place to be from;
It's kind to most, but cruel to some.

Now where on earth could this place be
That meant so much to you and me!?

-A Spiritual Paradox-

Being a slave seems a bitter thing,
But grasping for self the opposite brings;
The more we labor ourselves to enhance,
The more we lose that very chance.

If you would save your soul today,
Then you must give yourself away;
For only the love on others you cast
Will be the thing in your life that will last.

The power of Jesus to rise again
Was the love He gave to forgive our sin.
So follow His path that the world has not known,
And the soul that He saves will be your own!

-A Worthy Gift-

What's in a gift that gives it worth
As God deems value up above?
It's not how much it costs on earth,
But how much it's endowed with love.

It's not a gift when we demand
An equal one for what we've made;
No, that is not a helping hand;
For that is nothing but a trade.

The worth of what we truly give
Is not expecting in return,
For God gives us the grace to live
That none of us can ever earn.

Yes, God grants us not what He owes
'Cause there is nothing we have done
For the gifts to friends and foes
That He gives us through His Son.

Are our gifts not seen as hallowed?
Do we count that a disgrace
When our good deeds may be valued
As most would an ugly face?

So sometimes we treat God's treasure,
But He blesses just the same;
Gracious gifts beyond all measure
Come to us in Jesus' Name!

Thus, like God, let's view our gift,
Not by what folks may deserve;
But may we their burdens lift
As with Christ we humbly serve.

Then our gift will be of worth
As God sees it up above,
For He'll know our gift on earth
Is endowed with grace and love!

-Awake-

Awake, you souls,
Who sleep in death;
Now heed the Lord
And what he saith,

For you are dead
Today in sin
With only lifeless
Bones within.

But God would raise you
From your tomb
And save you from
Eternal doom.

But from your sin
You must repent
And trust in Christ
Whom God has sent.

So in His precious
Name believe,
And life through Him
You will receive.

Choose life, not death,
My friends, this day;
For He is but
A prayer away!

-Bitter-Sweet-

The Word of the Lord is just as sweet
As honey that drips from the comb;
But many refuse to hear God's voice,
And its sweetness remains unknown.

There are others who listen to what God says
But reject their chance to live,
For they love their sin too much to receive
The blessings that God would give.

How hard it is to die to self
And repent of iniquity;
There are simply those who foolishly choose
Bitter death as their destiny.

Yes, some do embrace God's gift of love,
And His Word is sweet to their taste;
But others insist on their own selfish wish,
And for them what Christ did is a waste,

Then the Son of God who gave Himself
So none of us mortals need die
Can only stand in the back of the church
With a heart-broken tear in His eye.

On a lonely hill called Calvary
Is where love and sorrow meet,
But only some embrace God's Son
So His gift is bitter-sweet.

Yes, some accept and others reject;
We know that this is true.
But looking deep in your soul today
In what group, my friend, are you?!

-Breathe The Name of Mother-

Breathe the name of mother;
Say it like a prayer;
Touch her in your memories,
And she will be there.

Breathe the name of mother;
Sense her presence near;
Hear her lilts of laughter,
Soft upon your ear.

Breathe the name of mother;
For she gave you breath,
Sharing all her moments
Til she had none left.

Breathe the name of mother;
Glimpse her now above;
She will like a magnet
Draw you with her love.

Breathe the name of mother;
Know she cares for you;
She's at peace with Jesus;
You can know it too.

Breathe the name of mother;
Whisper of her worth;
Make her proud she bore you
Here upon this earth.

Breathe the name of mother;
Do it while you may,
No better time to do it
Than on this Mother's Day!

-Broken-

Never on this earth below
Have truer words been spoken
Than an egg is only good
When it has been broken.

If its shell remains intact,
What good can it be?
It must first be opened wide
To nourish you and me.

So it was upon a cross
God to us has spoken;
And before His goodness flowed,
First His heart was broken.

Also, we with hardened hearts,
Festering sore with sin,
First must have them broken so
The Saviour can come in.

For no healing can take place
'Til shattered is our shell;
Only then can He in love
Make our spirits well.

So when God would bring to us
Wounded, broken hearts,
Know it is His goodness that
He to us imparts.

For it's true there are some things
Of which it is spoken
That can never be quite right
'Til they've first been broken!

-Come Back to Jesus-

O foolish lepers
Why do you laugh,
Content with a healing
That's only a half?

Why are you happy
With God's second best?
Come back to Jesus
And really be blest!

God's earthly healings
Truly are fine,
But so many lepers
Also are blind.

Come back to Jesus;
Be thankful and smart,
Not healed just in body
But also in heart!

O foolish nine,
Your flesh He'll restore;
But Christ wants to give you
A whole lot more!

Why do you settle
For less than the whole?
Healed in your body
But not in your soul.

O foolish lepers,
Nine out of ten,
Now you'll never know
What you might have been!

-Freedom's Flag-

Our freedom's enemies abound
And cast Old Glory to the ground,
But patriots have always been
So quick to raise our flag again.

Oh, may our colors always wave,
Lifting spirits of the brave
Who give themselves to their last breath,
Defending freedom to the death.

Though we may fall, we always rise
To lift our flag unto the skies,
And our Creator we will bless
For His unfailing faithfulness.

Yes, though we're threatened by our foes,
We will not yield an inch to those
Who turn our freedoms and our trust
Into cruel missites back at us.

Let's hoist the standard of our God,
And by His power protect the sod
That He entrusts into our care
And keep it always flying there.

O neighbors, sense your oneness now;
And share this noble, sacred vow
That you will always faithful be
To God's great gift of liberty!

Remember all who gave their lives
In selfless deeds of sacrifice;
Yea, may their memory shine bright
And help us overcome the night

Until all terrorists are gone,
And right has overcome the wrong;
Let's keep the faith until the day
All evil has been swept away.

Now as we mourn our nation's loss,
May we with courage pay the cost,
And glorify our Lord above
Supplanting terror with His love!

O freedom's flag, unfurl and flow;
And when it's time for us to go
To stand before God's Judgement Seat
And our Creator there to meet,

May we present our flag to Him
That represents what we have been;
To every freedom's faithful son,
May God declare, "My child, well done!"

-Forgiven-

When we have found folks let us down
And teardrops fill the eye,
With heavy care we go to prayer
And seek the reason, why?

Through every test, we've done our best
To help our mortal kin,
Then why would they our love repay
By grieving us within?

In deepest prayer our spirits share
Our sorrow and our woe:
We feel betrayed by wounds they made,
But why we want to know.

We trusted them, and yet they sin
By giving us their scorn;
Why would they test our faithfulness
And cause our souls to mourn?

Then in our hearts the Lord imparts
This thought to me and you,
And we're aware the cross we bear
Is like the one He knew.

He gave us love from Heaven above,
And yet we gave to Him
Not thankful souls but heavy woes
And selfishness of sin.

And as we gaze, we are amazed
The pain our sins have cost;
And in despair we see Him there
Upon a rugged cross!

Then in His tears, we see as mirrors
Our cross that others cause,
And yet the one we gave God's Son
Reveals our human flaws.

In spite of all, I hear His call,
My sins He will forgive;
Though great they be, He pardons me
So I in Him may live.

O help me, Lord, whom I adore,
Like you be truly meek;
And when again my neighbor sin
To turn the other cheek.

My precious Lord, I can't afford
To shun my enemy
Because I know within my soul
That you've forgiven me!

-First Church-

When your church
Is feeling blue,
Here is something
You can do.

Think of First Church
Christ began
Back in old Jerusalem.

The Session they
Had long ago
Felt their spirits
Very low.

Pastor Jesus
Soon was lost,
Dying on
A rugged cross.

Peter Clerk,
Afraid to die,
Would his pastor
Christ deny.

Suicide
The treasurer bore
After he
Betrayed his Lord.

All the Session
On that day
From their pastor
Ran away.

Just a few
From W.A.
Had fortitude
to stay.

Even they
Were so depressed,
They thought they
Had nothing left.

But in spite
Of all their woes,
First Church from
Its ashes rose.

Like their pastor,
Back from death,
They had new life,
Like He saith.

On them did
His Spirit rest;
Then it was
They did their best.

Proudly did
They carry on;
Peter, Mary,
James and John.

Thousands flocked
To join First Church
That had been left
In the lurch.

So if your church
May seem dead,
Think about
New life instead.

For when things
The darkest seem,
You are closest
To your dream.

Closer than
You ever knew
To your church dream
Coming true!

-First-

It's better to be first than last
When running in a race;
And it feels good to beat the throw
When rushing to first base.

But what is first with us below
Upon this earth of sod
In Heaven where it really counts
May not be first with God.

For what is really first with Him
In Heaven up above
Is not to put our own selves first
But other folks in love.

Yes, let us seek to act like Christ;
And when this life is past,
We'll find that we'll be first with God
Instead of being last!

-Egg Shells-

Broken eggs are good to savor,
Scrambled, they're a great delight;
But when bits of shell still linger,
They're not pleasing to the bite.

Yes, with broken hearts forgiven,
There is much for us to gain;
But if bits of self still linger,
Then our pleasure turns to pain.

Jesus leads us by example,
For He did it all before;
On a cross His heart was broken,
Showing love we can't ignore.

Oh, what grace in Christ, our Saviour,
Emptied of all self is He;
Not a single bit of egg shell
Mars His gift to you and me.

As we gaze on our Redeemer
Who bestows on us His best;
For us He renounced all egg shells,
How can we for Him do less?

Let us all in Christ endeavor
To be rid of what is hard,
For there's only joy in Jesus
When all egg shells we discard!

-Don't Be Afraid-

Don't be afraid
In the dead of night
When the angel of God
In a blaze of light
Appears to you
In glory's glow
And bids you
On a mission go.

Don't be afraid
When he asks of you
To do what he knows
God wants you to,
The challenge for which
You were placed on earth,
A chance at last
To prove your worth.

Don't be afraid,
Though you know you're weak;
For God will provide
The strength you seek.
Just trust the Lord,
To Him be true,
And the angel of God
Will go with you.

Don't be afraid
Of what others say
Who choose to go
In a different way.
Just keep in mind
At the setting sun,

You'll give an account
For what you've done.

If you do today
What God bids you do,
Then when your time
On earth is through,
There'll be no fear
For the Lord will say
"Well done!" to you
On Judgement Day.

This Christmas now
Cast out your fears
When the angel of God
To you appears.
Just seek His Son
And you will know
What shepherds learned
So long ago.

You too will find
God will impart
A special blessing
In your heart,
And that by grace
You'll find in you
That Jesus has
Been born anew!

Don't be afraid
In this world of night
When the angel comes
And gives you light.
Just heed his word

When he calls your name
And your life
Will never be the same!

-Don't Be Afraid-

Don't be afraid
That your life shall end,
But that it has
No beginning;
For you have died
A long time ago
It you love
To keep on sinning.

Christ won't save you
In your sins,
But from them
He will do.
For what you ask
From God above
The Lord will give
To you!

-Beware-

Beware of what you ask for
And what you will believe;
For what you ask is what you'll get
And what you will receive!

-God Meets Us-

When it is Good Friday,
God meets us at the cross;
There through Christ, our Saviour,
He seeks and saves the lost.

But with Easter's dawning,
When our darkness turns to day,
God meets us in a garden;
And He wipes our tears away.

Graveyards are for dying;
They're meant for bones and tombs;
But gardens are for living
Midst the flowers and their blooms.

Now embrace your Jesus
And the love that He imparts;
This is Easter Sunday,
And God meets us in our hearts!

-God's Best Gifts-

It's not so much
That God has need
Our human treasures
To receive.

But God's best gifts
That help us live
Are opportunities
To give.

For as we give
Ourselves in love,
We are the most
Like God above!

Yes, every gift
Will shape the soul
Of him who gives
Himself below!

-God Bless America-

What can bless our needy nation?
What can feed its hungry heart?
What can quench its thirsty spirit?
What can God to us impart?

He has blessed us so with riches,
Things we yearn for, things we crave,
Things of this world in abundance
That we must leave at the grave.

Sometimes what we think are blessings
Are but curses in disguise;
Then we find we are so foolish
When we thought we were so wise!

Bless America, our Father,
With the blessings that are true;
Help up die to selfish pleasure;
Help us to be more like You!

Jesus gave His life on Calv'ry,
Gave His Body and His Blood
To redeem us from the blessings
That in error we thought we loved.

So now lead us by Your Spirit
To the Table that is true
That by grace and faith in Jesus
We can all be born anew!

Then instill us with the blessing
That inspires us to share
And ourselves to be a blessing

To a nation in despair.

Bless America, our Father,
With the blessing that is true;
Fill us with the love of Jesus
That will make us more like you!

-I'll Be A Carpenter-

As Jesus prepared to leave Heaven,
He was asked what He would do
On earth until His time had come
And His mission there was through.

"I'll be a carpenter," He said,
"And work with wood and tool;
I'll fashion yokes and wagon wheels
With saw, and chisel, and rule.

My hands will work with the cedar
And shape the form of the pine
'Til at last I'll spread them on a cross
And save those I know to be mine.

From the dead limb of an old rugged cross,
I'll create a living tree,
And bring to life all those who repent
And put their faith in me.

Yes, I will be a carpenter there;
And by the power of my hand,
I'll take poor souls that are dead in sin
And make them to live again!"

-I Shall Wear Purple-

When I am old and turning gray,
I shall wear purple every day;
A royal color, it shall bring
Sweet memories of Christ, my King.

And when I'm old, I shall recall
The greatest memory of them all;
The vine's sweet fruit and what it meant,
God's only Son from Glory sent
To die upon a rugged tree,
To die for you and die for me.

Yes, when I'm old and turning gray,
I shall wear purple every day;
And when I reach fair Heaven's shore,
I shall wear purple evermore!

-I Have Within-

I have within my soul today
A haunting , godly fear;
It warns me of my sinful self
That lingers ever near.

But then the Holy Spirit speaks
And grants me grace to know
That I must seek the Saviour's will
And yield to His control!

O stubborn heart that still rebels,
Let go of that which burns;
For Christ can slay the savage beast
Which to the Saviour turns.

Seek now the peace that Jesus Christ
Will to the sinner give,
And sense the awesome power of love
And what it means to live!

-Holy Week-

With Hosanna sound, He rode into town
With His trusty colt and crew;
Just why He came in Messiah's name
The ignorant crowd never knew.

Their garments were laid and the palms were waved
In the honor of their King;
But as they cheered, His enemies feared
The threat to them He would bring.

They knew they were right when they then caught sight
Of Jesus wearing a frown;
In the Temple there that was meant for prayer,
They defiled His hold ground.

So He kicked their chairs, tipped over their wares,
And threw them into the dirt;
Then He whipped them bad like no one had
And gave them a terrible hurt.

This Temple brood in a manner rude
Took offense to what Christ said;
In a way uncouth they spurned His truth
And plotted to see Him--dead!

A trap of lies spelled His demise
As the nails they hammered in;
Unrecognized He agonized
On a cross to forgive their sin.

If they only knew, this motley crew,
T'was for them He died on that tree;
But in their pride they brushed aside
The love they just wouldn't see.

Instead their sin they kept within,
In arrogance sealing their fate;
Not knowing this One was God's only Son,
And now it was too late.

But for those who believed and His grace received,
He planned a special surprise,
For on the 3rd day in a wondrous way
From the grave did the Saviour arise!

Yes, one day so bold on a colt He rode
On the way to His destiny;
So many back then preferred their sin,
But how about you and me?

-Hezekiah-

Hezekiah was a man
Serving God the best he can.

All the time the king was well,
He was good and things were swell.

But the king began to cry
When it came his time to die.

Hezekiah was upset,
For he wasn't ready yet

To leave earthly things behind;
So, behold, God changed His mind!

To the king the Lord did give
Fifteen more years he could live.

But the king, whom God had blessed,
Loved things more, and served God less.

Longer life became a curse,
And things went from bad to worse.

So this moral we should know;
When God calls, it's time to go!

Yes, sometimes things work out best,
Not with more years, but with less.

So when life has passed you by -a,
Just remember Hezekiah!

-Inside Christ's Church-

What joy to step inside Christ's Church
To listen, sing, and pray;
The Holy Spirit touches me
And takes my sins away.

I feel that in these sacred walls
My soul is born anew,
And I am clearer in my mind
What God would have me do.

There is no sweeter fellowship
Than in God's holy place;
The Presence of the living Lord
Shines from each smiling face.

I drink the cup of sacrifice
And eat the bread of love;
By faith I am transported
To a higher plane above.

And as I leave this hallowed home,
The Word of God I heed,
Prepared to give myself away
To others now in need!

-Incarnation-

There's nothing that we like so much
As what our fingertips can touch;
And nothing has the same appeal
As what our own two hands can feel.

So when it comes to the Deity,
How great it is for you and me
When God appeared in a human form
And as a baby boy was born.

How thankful we are for the shape God's in,
As tender and warm as a baby's skin,
A wonderful form for the blessed Christ
Who came to be our sacrifice!

-In the Wake-

In the wake of troubled waters
Churned upon this mortal sea
By the passing of a vessel
That brought joy to you and me.

There remains in swirling whirlpools
On the surface of the deep
Blessed memories of a loved one
That within our hearts we keep.

Even now off in the distance
We can see his sailboat's light
There beyond the rolling breakers
In the darkness of the night.

In our minds we'll see forever
Loring's ship unfurled of sail
As with skill and dauntless courage,
He faced sunny skies and gale.

There was great strength in his rigging
That brought many through the storm,
And the love he shared with others
Kept his cabin bright and warm.

There was laughter 'broad his vessel
As he spun a tale or two;
He was honest with his shipmates
And was generous with his crew.

Now at last he rests in harbor
With the Captain of his soul
Who through heavy seas has guided

Loring safely by the shoal.

Yes, his voyage now is over,
Anchored firm by Heaven's shore,
Where his soul finds peace and comfort
With the Lord forevermore.

So let not your hearts be troubled;
Trust your Captain at the wheel.
He has sailed here long before us,
And he knows just how we feel.

Thank you, Jesus, for Your solace
As you wipe away each tear,
For our dear departed shipmate
And the time we knew him here.

Yes, we thank you for our memory
Of his mortal journey done;
And we know that we shall see him
At the setting of our sun.

In the wake of troubled waters
Churned upon this mortal sea,
We ponder all this sailor's life
Has meant to you and me!

-In the Valley-

In the valley of the shadow,
There my Shepherd comes to me;
At the gathering gloom of twilight,
Haunting my mortality.

But the Shepherd, kind and gentle,
Puts His hand within my own;
And with tender love and mercy
Leads my needy spirit home.

In His Presence fear and doubting
Melt away like snow in spring;
And through gardens filled with flowers,
I can hear the angels sing.

Other souls that turned to cinders
I find littered on the way,
Cursed by worship of the Mammon
Drained all their life away.

But I died to worldly idols
That I knew would let me down,
And instead embraced the Shepherd,
Trading trinkets for a crown.

Hand in hand I walk with Jesus
Through death's dirge of deepest night
Til at last my journey's over,
And my faith is turned to sight.

Precious Prince of power and pardon,
You in pity paid my price;
And now by your grace and glory
Usher me to Paradise.

Oh, what joy to know the Shepherd
As the dawn breaks in the east,
For eternity awaits me
In the land of perfect peace.

There I'll sip of Canaan's waters,
And I'll sup on manna's fare;
Most of all I'll be with Jesus
And be never wanting there.

Loving Shepherd, I will laud you
Throughout Heaven's endless days,
And I'll find my greatest pleasure
Singing songs of ceaseless praise!

-In the Garden-

In the garden Jesus came
Calling Mary by her name.

She was weeping for the dead,
But she found her Lord instead

Was alive to meet her there
In the garden of her prayer.

So we gather here to tell
Her we love a fond farewell.

Tears of grief down cheeks may flow,
For in truth we love her so.

But come not to seek the dead,
For she is alive instead.

To her spirit Jesus came,
And He called to her by name.

Yes, the Way, the Truth, the Life
Met our mother, friend, and wife

In the garden we can't see
To fulfill her destiny.

Though our bodies here may fade,
We are in God's image made;

And through Jesus is it true,
We are made to live anew!

So have faith in Christ, my friend;
For our loved one lives again.

And someday we all shall come
In the garden of the Son.

Then He'll call us each by name,
And we'll never be the same.

For in love He takes His own
To His lovely garden home

Where our loved ones we shall see
Throughout all eternity.

In the garden Jesus came;
Let us bless His holy Name!

-Hair-

Don't worry when your hair falls out;
Instead feel great relief.
Just think of all the pain you miss
'Cause hair's not like your teeth!

For teeth grow old, and painfully
They're pulled out for your health;
But when it's time for hair to go,
It does so by itself!

Hairs bear no grudge and cause no ache;
They're gone in just a wink:
One moment they're upon your head,
The next, they're in your sink.

So thank your hair for what it does
And what it doesn't do;
For though your teeth may treat you mean,
Your hair is good to you!

So when you see your hair fall out,
Just smile in great relief;
And think of all the pain you miss
'Cause hair's not like your teeth!

-Grace-

We don't pray for mercy, Lord;
Justice will condemn our soul.
We need something over which
We in sin have no control.

If you give us what is fair,
Horrible will be our fate.
May we realize this truth
Now before it is too late.

Pride and arrogance insist
Seeking what they feel their due;
But if this we would demand,
Pain and death will come from you.

As we kneel before your throne,
Nought of goodness can we bring.
Evil dwells within our hearts
Saturating everything.

We must have what we can't claim;
It is yours to keep or give.
Will you grant us from your love
What our spirits need to live?

We are undeserving, Lord;
Grace is what we crave from Thee.
Only grace can meet our need
Throughout all eternity.

So we seek for grace, O Lord;
There can be no other way.
Only by your grace in Christ
Can you take our sins away.

Fill us with your Presence, Lord;
May your Spirit overflow
Until souls in all the earth
Grace within their beings know!

-Jesus Saves-

So what does it profit
A man on this earth
To gain the whole world
That's of so little worth?

And why do we even
Bother to boast
When we lose the one thing
That matters the most?

For what foolish things
Are we tempted to trade
In exchange for the soul
Our Creator has made?

Yes , we pamper the body,
Neglecting the soul;
To forces of darkness
We yield its control.

We squander our choices
On trinkets of dust,
On things that decay
And on things that will rust.

Then when all the lights
On this earth have gone out,
We have nothing left
But our fears and our doubt.

So what can we do
In view of our plight
To escape all the heartaches
Of eternal night?

There is only One
Who can ever impart
New life to the soul
And true love to the heart.

So focus on Jesus
And what He can give,
For He alone has
What our soul needs to live.

But we can't serve the world
And also serve Him;
We have to serve God,
Or we have to serve sin.

This power of choice
May be something we loathe,
But we have to pick one,
For we cannot serve both.

So let us determine
Which way we will go;
Yet there is one thing
That we all need to know:

That only Christ Jesus
Has power o'er the grave,
And only the Lord
Has the power to save!

-Jonah-

Jonah was an Israelite
And from God got a call
To preach to heathen Ninevites
About to take a fall.

But Jonah didn't like those folks
So went down to the bay
And hopped aboard a sailing boat
That cruised the other way.

But God sent lightning, wind and rain
That was a mighty gale;
And Jonah plunging in the sea
Was swallowed by a whale!

Three days and lonely nights went by
Upon the ocean floor
Until God caused the whale to spit
Poor Jonah on the shore.

At last he did what he was told
And helped the folks repent;
He could have done it earlier
If only he had went.

Just think of all that Jonah bore
Because he ran away;
So let us learn from Jonah's plight,
And do God's will today!

-Lemons-

When we find life is one, big mess,
Just realize that God knows best;
For faith will grow and troubles fade,
And God will make us lemonade!

Don't envy one who seems too blessed,
For what seems much is really less;
Just take the chance your lemons give,
And God will teach you how to live!

Yes, what seem objects of despair,
By means of faith and loving prayer,
Will be the very means you need
For God to help you to succeed!

-Like Ripening Corn-

A Christian is like ripening corn,
Or so a wise man said:
The riper that each of them grows,
The more he bows his head!

Thus, let us like the ripening corn
Now bow our heads in prayer;
And as we pray for those in need,
We'll find the Lord is there.

Yes, though it's hard to get to church,
At home we still can pray,
And know within our deepest souls
God's just a prayer away.

So as our bodies bend with age
And lower toward the earth,
It is with joy we realize
How much our prayers are worth!

-Like Oatmeal-

Our souls are so like oatmeal
That we prepare on earth,
A treasure beyond measure,
Undervalued in its worth.

We place it in a microwave
And then turn on the heat,
But cooking without looking
Makes it unfit to eat.

When we leave oatmeal on its own,
It isn't for the best;
Those boiling bubbles cause us troubles
And make a nasty mess.

We try to scoop the oatmeal back
And overcome its curse;
But when we do, I'm telling you,
We only make things worse!

We simply cannot get it all
Into the bowl again;
We've made a mess we must confess,
And so it is with sin.

The heat of tribulation
Is needed for our souls,
But be aware without due care
They're soon beyond control.

For we're distracted by this world,
And that is most unwise;
Yes, more or less we make a mess
Before we realize.

And by the time we understand
The awful state we're in,
It's just too late to change our fate
And save ourselves from sin.

We need the Saviour from above
Who cleans up all our stains,
For He'll impart a brand new heart
So none of them remains.

He gives us each another chance;
It's up to me and you.
It we believe, we will receive
The grace to start anew.

We need the heat of troubles here,
But let the truth be known
That if we trust the Lord in us,
We need not cope alone.

For He will help us face each test
And grow each day within
Until at last all trials pass
And we're in Heaven with Him.

Yes, souls are so like oatmeal;
I tell you this, my friend,
When we prepare them both with care,
They'll bless us in the end!

-Like Water Into Wine-

Jesus went to Cana,
A town in Galilee;
He went to bless a wedding
Like He blesses you and me.

He took some common water,
The ordinary kind;
And by His love and power,
He changed it into wine.

So Jesus Christ can take us,
Though common we may be,
And by His grace and mercy
Can change both you and me.

So let us simply trust Him,
And we will surely find
That we will all be miracles,
Like water into wine!

-Memorial Day Prayer-

Our God, who art in Heaven,
On this Memorial Day,
We turn from all the things of earth
And take the time to pray.

For those who've gone before us
And given us their all
In answer to a needy world
And to their country's call.

We thank you for their service,
And may we too be true
As we remember what they did
Our freedoms to renew.

Impress upon our play-proned minds
Each day, we humble ask,
That we may sense the urgency
Of our appointed task.

To look beyond the god of self
That we in love may give
Ourselves away like those who died
So other men might live.

We seek not for less work to do,
For many need our care;
We only ask for strength from you
So we can do our share..

Grant us compassion, gracious God,
For those whose souls we feed,
Especially for those so blind
They cannot see their need,

We know that if our work is slack,
Then great will be the cost;
And freedoms we have cherished so
May be forever lost.

Yes, gracious Father, whom we trust,
We know our prayers are heard;
We only seek like those before
To have the chance to serve.

And when this passing life is o'er,
May we hear deep within
Those glorious words, "Well done, my child!"
In Jesus' Name, Amen!

-Memory-

Memory is a treasure chest
We add to day by day
With precious jewels that we collect
Along life's pilgrim way.

And then at special times like these,
We'll take a gem or two
And think about the days gone by
And loved ones we once knew.

How precious are those memories
That in our minds we see;
How wonderful as we recall
Just how things used to be.

Sometimes the memories that come
Will bring with them a tear,
And sometimes they bring laughter
From a long past yesteryear.

So now let's thank our loving Lord
For memories He may give
And know through them within our hearts
Our loved one still can live!

-Minutemen For Jesus-

Minutemen for Jesus,
Harken to My call;
Minutemen for Jesus
Come and give your all!

But we only whimper,
Someone else, not I;
Choose another soldier,
I don't want to die!

Sadly Christ is crying
As He shakes His head;
Although you don't know it,
You're already dead!

Feasting on the world's food,
You've grown soft inside,
Down deep in your spirit,
Long ago you died.

My bread you have squandered;
My cup you have spilled.
You preferred the meal of men,
With it you are filled.

Yet now at My Table
Is My bread and wine;
You can have another chance
To be truly mine.

For I gave My body,
And I shed My blood;
If you will receive them,

You will live in love.

Cast away your idols,
And repent of sin;
Then by grace from Heaven,
You'll be born again!

Come and be My soldiers,
Minutemen of Mine;
You will be My branches;
I will be your vine.

Enemies you'll conquer
And My power within,
And you'll be victorious
Over every sin.

Minutemen for Jesus,
Harken to My call;
Minutemen for Jesus,
Come and give your all!

-Monuments-

In our lives we're building
Our monuments each day;
We add a stone with every deed
And every word we say.

What is it that we're building
For our eternity,
Something that is lovely, or
A pile of debris?

How will we be remembered
When all is said and done?
Will each rock be a stone of self,
Or love for everyone?

Will they bring God's blessing,
Or will they cause His wrath?
Will others point to them with pride,
Or will they simply laugh?

Yes, when this life is over,
Our monuments will be
For good or ill how we'll be known
Throughout eternity.

Our monuments we're building,
So let us all beware;
And let us all be certain
That we're building them with care!

-Mountains-

I climb mountains
'Cause I found them;
That's why others
Go around them.

What to them
A barrier seems
Is the answer
To my dreams.

The obstacle
That others see
To me's
An opportunity!

Thank you, Lord,
For mountains tall;
How sad if there
Were none at all.

To the mountains
I belong,
For it's they
That make me strong.

God gives mountains
For the finding,
And I praise Him
For the climbing!

-Prayer-

Prayer can be as quiet
As the calm before the storm
When nature hushed in silence waits
For power to be born.

Prayer can be in crying
As mirth or sorrow spent,
A human soul's most inward thought
By saltine rivers sent.

Prayer can be as rousing
As the drums and pipes of war;
Prayer can energize within
And make us yearn for more.

Prayer can be a blessing
That fills the heart with joy;
Prayer can be the greatest gift
A mortal can employ.

But prayer can be a chasm,
As wide as it can be;
Prayer can be aborted, friends,
By folks like you and me.

Tragic are unanswered prayers;
They seem like they are dead.
Far greater is the tragedy
Of prayers we left unsaid.

Yes, with prayer it's often true
We're so prone to abuse it
When in faithfulness we fall
And we refuse to use it!

-Promises-

Our promises are special things
That we should always keep,
For broken promises are sad
And always make us weep.

But there is One who promises
And always keeps His word;
And from the Holy Bible,
God's promises are heard.

He promises to be with us
And meet our every need;
If we in turn will do His will,
He'll help us to succeed.

And when this life on earth is done,
If we are true to Him,
Then God will keep His word to us;
And Heaven we will win.

Have faith in God who loves you so;
In Him now put your trust,
For He will keep all promises
That He has made to us.

Yes, let us all be more like God
With promises we make,
And life for us, and others too,
Will then be truly great!

-Qanna-

Qanna's a most peculiar word;
And though it may sound quite absurd,
It means both zeal and jealous too;
Which one depends on me and you.

God gives emotions deep within
That we can use for good or sin;
So if we use it selfishly,
Then qanna becomes jealousy.

But if it's perfect love we feel,
Then qanna in our hearts is zeal;
Yes, qanna can be wrong or right,
So let's use ours as Jesus might.

Be zealous for your fellow man;
Do all for others that you can,
For love with zeal can set us free
From every trace of jealousy.

-Remember-

Those who don't remember
The errors of days gone by
Are prone just to repeat them
As future days draw nigh.

And those who do remember
The good things of the past
By keeping memories alive
Will help those good things last!

-The Commandments of Christ-

We live in a world
Where there's always a voice
That rejects what Christ says
With an easier choice.

But some day you wake up
And find that it's true
That the someone who pays
Is no one but you!

At your table of life,
Many folks eat their fill;
But you are the one
Who is stuck with the bill!

So listen to Jesus
And heed His demands,
For His love for you
Is behind His commands.

And if you obey,
Then it will be known
That the soul He saves
Will be your own!

Commandments seem heavy
And so hard to bear,
But Jesus is with you
The burden to share.

So give Him your all;
In love sacrifice,
And you'll find what you give
Will surely suffice!

-The Lost Awe-

America, what has become
Of us whom God has blessed?
Have we been spoiled by our wealth
And failed to meet the test?

Adversity we seem to face
And triumph valiantly;
But how have we responded, friends,
To our prosperity?

Where is the awe we owe our Lord;
What god is worshipped now?
How could we be so foolish
As to break our sacred vow?

Amusement parks and shopping malls
Are filled with swarming throng;
But empty pews in silence cry,
"God's worshippers are gone!"

In patience has our rightful Lord
Endured His people's scorn;
And God proclaims, "America,
You need to be reborn!"

Yes, let us now return to God;
Give awe that's due His Name.
Let darkened churches shine again
With Heaven's holy flame.

But if we shun the Master's call
And if we wait too late,
Some day He will withdraw His hand

And leave us to our fate.

So when we pass our darkened church,
Where once the light we saw,
Let's know the candle flickered out
Because we lost the awe.

The awe of God , reclaim it, friends,
While we still have the time;
For if we truly reverence God,
His glory we will find.

Just think of awe this church has known
And awe that might have been;
For when at last our chance is passed,
The awe won't come again!

-The Measure-

It's not how you die
But how you live,
Not what you get
But what you give.

Yes, there are ways
To measure your worth
No matter how low
Or how high your birth.

It's not your shrine,
Or even your creed;
But have you befriended
Another in need.

It's not when you die
What the newspapers say,
But if folks were sorry
That you passed away.

Yes, it makes no difference
Your status at birth,
But how you live
Determines your worth.

For though man judges
Your outward part,
The Lord looks only
Upon your heart!

-The Church-

I like to come into the Church
And meet with Jesus there;
I bow my head in deepest awe
And share with Him my prayer.

All fear and doubt are swept aside,
My spirit is at rest;
For I am in my Father's house,
And I am greatly blessed.

And as I give my heart to Him,
I sense the Lord above
Redeeming me from all my sin
And filling me with love.

Yes, as I leave this sacred place,
Beyond its walls to trod,
I'll always carry in my heart
The precious love of God!

-The Believer's Judgement-
I Cor. 3:10-15

What do we all plan to do today?
What will last or pass away?
Sensing this should give us pause
When we choose our daily cause.

For the Day when we retire,
God will test our works by fire;
Even for the Christian man;
'Fore the Bema he must stand.

And account for all his deeds,
Whether they be wheat or weeds;
Then in truth we will behold
Whether they be dross or gold.

Will the treasures that we choose
Be the ones we keep or lose?
Will the deeds of all our days
Be survivors of God's blaze?

So be careful , Christian friend,
For your life on earth will end;
Choose to do now what is best,
And you'll pass the final test.

Of the flames that are to come
On the altar of God's Son;
Choose now wisely what you do,
And your works will honor you!

-Strangers-

How sad, dear Christ, that we should be
Such strangers to each other;
O, that God were our Father, Lord,
And I Thy younger brother.

How blessed it would be to walk
Down life's bleak, wintry road;
The warmth of love that we could share
Would shield us from the cold.

Yes, we could talk of Heaven's things
Through fair and stormy weather,
Assured no matter what might come
That we would be together.

This sweet communion others, Lord,
In spirit have with Thee;
O, how my soul yearns deep within
That you'd have it with me!

Reveal Thyself to me, I pray
And put Thy hand in mine,
That in this time of special need
Thy comfort I may find.

No longer be a stranger, Lord,
But be my faithful Friend;
In turn I will be true to Thee
And love Thee to the end!

-To Give Is To Live-

We make a living by what we get,
But when we do, we're not there yet;
We make a life by what we give;
Yes, only then we learn to live.

And what we get we all must lose,
Not knowing this will make us fools;
So let us spend our whole life giving,
For that's the key to really living.

We only keep what we each day,
In love for others give away;
This truth we learn from God above,
Who gave Himself for us in love!

-To Wait, Too Late-

Today's the time that we create
Our memories for tomorrow,
And chances we let pass us by
Our future cannot borrow.

So let us do what we can do
For loved ones here today
Before the sands of time run out
And sadly slip away.

Let's say that word we ought to say
And never speak the bad;
Let's do the loving deed right now
And make another glad.

Yes, give the flowers here and now
While other folks can see them,
For they're more precious while we live
Than in our mausoleum.

Let's do the very best we can,
And memories will be
A treasure in the future
To be shared by you and me.

Yes, wisely use this present time,
For memories won't wait;
And there is nothing sadder
Than to know we are too late!

-Tomorowland-

There are no words that God can use
To help us fully understand
The glories that await His saints
In His divine tomorrowland.

What kind of mansions will there be,
What sort of place does Christ prepare,
What type of things shall we behold
When we at last are living there?

Faint glimpses of what God has planned
Do we in love from Him receive,
But they are clothed in imagery
And hard for our minds to perceive.

I'm sure the Lord would tell us more
If only we could comprehend
What He has willed for all of us
Who truly serve Him to the end.

For now we must be satisfied
By faith to serve God where we are,
Content to wait for our new home
And view it only from afar.

But one day time shall be no more;
Then we of Heaven's fruits shall taste,
And best of all we shall behold
Our loving Saviour face to face.

And what to us now is obscure
Will then we fully understand
And praise the Lord forevermore
In His divine tomorrowland!

-Wine or Whine?-

Little grapes are growing in
God's vineyard here today;
Some develop wondrously,
And some just fade away.

Some soak up the love of Christ
From both rain and sun,
And they'll make the finest wine
When the season's done.

Others only waste away
While they're on the vine,
Finding fault with this and that;
All they do is whine.

Whining is for the sinner, but
The wine is for the saint;
If you are the one, my friend,
The other one you ain't!

Whining saps us of our juice;
And on that occasion
When we're called to give account,
We'll only be a raisin.

In the likeness of the grape
We too are preparing
With a sour bit of whine,
Or sweet love we're sharing.

So within our hearts today,
Are we weak or brazen;
Does God see us prime with wine,
Or just a shriveled raisin?

-Who's Left-

It's not how many start with God
The race of life to run,
But who of us are true to Him
Until the race is won.

Yes, it's so easy just to quit,
But there's a better way;
For quitters can't be winners
No matter what they say.

So let us be what we must be
And do what we must do
To be among the winners when
The race of life is through.

And let us all remember what
The little poet saith:
It's not who starts the race with God,
But at the end, who's left!

-When-

When you're depressed
And feeling blue,
And no one else on earth
Loves you,

When trouble threatens
Everywhere,
And you know nothing
But despair,

When all your world
Has split apart
And left you with
A broken heart,

Then gaze again
Deep in your soul,
And you will be
Surprised to know

That if you'll look,
Yes, if you'll dare,
You'll find, my friend,
That God is there!

For He shines brightest
In our dark,
And it will only
Take one spark

For Him whose grace
Is great and true
To start a flame
Of love in you.

And when you pass
This flame around
To other troubled
Souls in town,

Then you'll discover
When you do,
This flame will stay
Alive in you.

For this is what
True love's about;
When it's not shared,
Then it goes out.

But when love's shared
By you and me,
Then it will last
Eternally!

-What's Right With The Church-

What's right with the Church?
I'll tell you true;
The Church has me,
And the Church has you!

To make this claim
May seem quite rash;
But God made us,
And He doesn't make trash!

Yes, He's given us life
And a job to do,
And He trusts in us
To see it through.

So when others try
To put us down,
And we're tempted in Church
To wear a frown,

Just keep in mind
That we're not our own;
We belong to Christ,
And we're not alone.

He provides His Church
From Heaven above
The heights of His power
And the depths of His love.

With the force of His Spirit
In me and in you,
There's nothing on earth
That His Church cannot do.

So let's get busy
And serve God's Son
'Til He comes again
And our work is done.

Then the Church triumphant
Will be His bride,
And His Spirit with us
Will forever abide.

Yes, let's make sure,
Whatever we do,
That the Church has me
And the Church has you!

-The Rope of Prayer-

Our prayer is like a belfry rope
That reaches to the sky;
And when we pull that rope below,
We ring God's bell on high.

The prayer of some of us is weak,
As we can plainly tell;
For there is little or no sound
That's coming from the bell.

Thus, let us pull the rope of prayer
With fervent faith this hour
So that the bell may sound aloud
With God's eternal power.

But first let us inspect the rope
That rises in our steeple
And make sure it's attached to God
And simply not to people.

For God won't answer any prayer
That's just a whim of man
No matter if that rope we pull
As firmly as we can.

So let us tie our rope to God
And yank it if we dare,
And then His bell will loudly sound
In answer to our prayer.

-The Ring of Love-

Love is a ring
That has no end;
It's greater than any
Thing else has been.

It's the essence of God,
The substance of life,
And the bond that binds
A husband and wife.

Yes, perfect love
Can overcome
And blend two spirits
Into one.

There is no truer
Power than this
For which a mortal
Could ever wish

Than the ring of love
That charms our hearts
And the matchless joy
That it imparts.

Sad is the soul
Whose fear and doubt
From the ring of love
Would keep him out.

But blest is he
Whose faith is strong;
To him does the ring
Of love belong.

Come, join the ring
Of love today,
And let God's Spirit
Have His way.

Then the ring of love
For you and me
Will be ours to share
Eternally!

-The New Song-

Let them keep their silence
Who do not know the Christ;
Only those the new song sing
Who share His sacrifice.

Let the world be muted,
Opiumed with sin;
Only those who die to self
Rise to sing again.

Hark unto the martyrs
Who leave death behind;
Only those in Jesus
Can redemption find.

Yes, when we're repentant
Totally of wrong,
Only then to Jesus
Do our souls belong.

We must fully trust Him
And in Him believe;
Only then salvation
Can our hearts receive.

Then we are awakened
From the sleep of doubt;
Every fear is vanquished,
Every sin cast out.

For we have a new song,
Which we gladly sing,
Of our soul's redemption
By our God the King.

There is none to fake it,
Though the masses try;
Yet their souls are empty,
And they wonder why.

But for us in Jesus
Who have paid the cost,
We who count for His sake
Everything as loss.

We give up what we can't keep,
This we gladly choose,
To accept new life in Christ
That we cannot lose.

Then He gives the new song
No one else can give;
We rejoice to sing it,
For our spirits live!

And with host of others
In the choir of grace,
We will sing in rapture,
Smiles upon our face.

Oh, how great the future
Jesus has in store;
Let us sing the new song
Now and evermore!

-The Meek-

We all are nearest Heaven when
We're furthest from self,
For meekness is the essence of
Our God's eternal wealth.

We all inherit Paradise
Who let go of our pride;
WHhn we embrace humility,
We find our Lord inside.

The truly meek among mankind
Will someday know their worth,
For it is they that Jesus said
Will one day own the earth.

Though tyrants now control this earth,
And dominate the weak,
One day the Lord will take it back
And give it to the meek.

How pitiful the souls of those
Who see themselves as God;
What good will be their power when
They lie beneath the sod?

All those of violent nature will
The good Lord sweep away,
And only meek and humble souls
Will be allowed to stay.

One day this world shall die in flames,
    And with it hate and fear;
A new one by the power of God
    Shall in its place appear.

Then God will give it to the meek,
    Who serve their Lord above;
And they shall rule the earth in peace
    And bless it with their love.

All meek souls know that Christ will come;
    They glory in the News,
For wise men give what they can't keep
    To gain what they can't lose!

-Of Holy Week-

There's so much we don't understand,
And there are those who never can
Look much beyond these mortal scenes
And comprehend what Jesus means.

We think of fleshly treasure first
And thereby suffer from its curse;
We mostly seek for this world's wealth,
And let our soul destroy itself.

But in this time of Holy Week,
We have a chance our Lord to seek.
Will we be foolish or be wise?
Will it bring life or our demise?

Let us think now what we will do
With this week given me and you;
Choose well, for it will soon be past;
And it, indeed, may be our last.

Will sun be ours, or will it fade
And cause to rain on our parade?
The choice is ours, both you and me;
We choose this week our destiny!

-True Friends-

True friends aren't jealous of your coups,
Or snicker when you fail;
And patiently they hear you out
When long may be your tale.

True friends don't ask how they can help;
In truth they simply know,
And then they do what they must do
To really help you grow.

Yes, when with friends you disagree
And argue through the night,
Then if they're true, they won't insist
That they have to be right.

True friends will overlook your faults,
And you will do the same;
Yes, true friends have no need to judge
And feel no urge to blame.

What true friends say behind your back,
They'll tell you to your face;
And claiming you a dearest friend
To them is no disgrace.

If on this earth true friends like these
The Lord to you has given,
Then gratitude should fill your soul,
For you are really livin'!

But if you want this kind of friend
Around you constantly,
Then know it is this kind of friend
That you yourself must be!

-Trampled Flowers-

Some may think of death as only
Being life that sours,
But to God it is the scent
Of lovely, trampled flowers.

Memories that grace our minds
Only can be ours
When death comes to those we love
Leaving trampled flowers.

There are tears of human grief
In these troubled hours;
Yet no perfume scent is known
Without trampled flowers.

Mortal petals on us all
Fall from Heaven's towers,
But we sense there's life anew
In these trampled flowers.

For the flesh must fade away
And release the powers
That God gives beyond this world
And its trampled flowers!

-Then How Much More?-

If Jesus felt the need to stay
Within God's house for days
So He could seek and find therein
The holy Father's ways,

The how much more I need to be
In Church where I can learn
So many things of God before
His will I can discern!

If Jesus on the Temple grounds
All other things forsook
To study and to talk about
The Father's sacred Book,

Then how much more within my life
Must I have need to read
The Holy Bible's pages and
Its blessed teachings heed!

If Jesus felt the urgent need
Within His soul to pray
So He could have the fellowship
And strength of God each day,

Then how much more my spirit needs
To have these blessings too
If I like Christ would have the pow'r
The Father's will to do!

If Jesus had to agonize
And had to bear a cross,
If He found that He had to count
All worldly things as loss,

Then how much more must I a
Mortal learn to do the same
If I'm to follow in His steps
And glorify God's name!

If it required of God's Son
The giving of His all
Before He could prepare Himself
To heed His Father's call,

Then how much more of one so frail
Like I must God demand
Before He thinks I'm ready
To become His businessman!

O let us give the Lord our lives
And to our God be true;
O let His spirit dwell within
So we can live anew.

Then how much more He'll say of us
Like He'll say of His Son
In Heaven when this life is o'ver,
"Well done, my child, well done!"

-The Wind's Travel-

Across this vast earth a silent wind blew--
It told of men's troubles and told them so true.
It told of man's war, his sin and his grief,
It told of the wise men, the beggar, and thief;
It told of each country in peace and in war,
It told of their greediness, greatness, and hoard.

"But all things on earth aren't as bad as they seem,"
Said the wind, with a sigh of relief.

Just think of the mountains, the trees, and the birds,
The rumbling rivers, and thundering herds,
The grain as it's blowing so free in the wind,
Just waiting for harvest to be gathered in.
Then softly the wind changes into a breeze,
And sounds like a murmur, as it goes through the trees.

-The Silent Saviour-

Like a sheep before the slaughter
And a lamb before the knife,
Our Saviour uttered not a word
To try to save His life.

Why would He not protest His fate;
Why utter not a word?
Though He in truth was innocent,
No cry from Him was heard.

Indeed, He was the Son of God,
The King of Heaven above;
But only being still could Christ
Most clearly speak His love.

He could have called His angels forth
To strike the sinners dead,
But Jesus chose to die for us
And save our souls instead.

Oh, how His silence did exclaim
Like words could never do,
The greatness of the love He had
Within for me and you.

And so He bore the crown of thorns,
Endured the soldier's lash;
In silence He picked up the cross
And carried out His task.

May we like Him in silence be
When others injure us;
Instead of vengeance, look to God,
And in Him put our trust.

For sometimes speech is hollow,
And by others is not heard;
But a deed of love in silence
Is much louder than a word!

-One Day A Year-

While looking at the calendar,
There's something I must say:
Why is there but one day a year
We call Thanksgiving Day?

So many humans spend their time
Complaining of their lot;
So many days they gripe to God
Of things that they have not.

But how much better it would be,
I boldly would suggest,
If we would have one Griping Day
And thank God all the rest!

-Not A Word-

Communications we hold dear,
A cell phone pressed to every ear;
We have a million things to say,
And yet we find it hard to pray.

To family, friends, and even foes,
We speak to everyone of those;
With non-stop voice we fill the air,
And yet we scarcely say a prayer.

Though we be old or we be young,
It seems the cat has got our tongue;
For though God's but a breath away,
We just can't find a things to say.

How sad our sounds can fill His sky,
While He is left to wonder why
By many others we are heard
And yet for Him we've not a word!

-I'll Be A Carpenter-

As Jesus prepared to leave Heaven,
He was asked what He would do
On earth until His time had come
And His mission there was through.

"I'll be a carpenter," He said,
"And work with wood and tool;
I'll fashion yokes and wagon wheels
With saw, and chisel, and rule.

My hands will work with the cedar
And shape the form of the pine
'Til at last I'll spread them on a cross
And save those I know to be mine.

From the dead limb of a old rugged cross,
I'll create a living tree,
And bring to life all those who repent
And put their faith in me.

Yes, I will be a carpenter there;
And by the power of my hand,
I'll take poor souls that are dead in sin
And make them to live again!"

-If Magi Had Been Women-

If Magi had been women
Instead of being guys,
Then those who came to Jesus
Would truly have been wise.

They would have come much sooner
Instead of two years late;
They'd stopped to ask directions,
A thing men seem to hate.

If Magi had been women,
They'd used the Triple A
Instead of trusting some strange star
To help them find their way.

They would have brought a casserole
And swept that stable clean;
They'd thrown the biggest baby shower
The world had ever seen.

How useless frankincense and myrrh;
A crib they'd given instead.
It would have been much better than
A smelly manger bed.

A baby doesn't care for gold
And knows no need for wealth;
Instead a pacifier would be placed
In Jesus' mouth.

If Magi had been women,
They'd surely babysit
So Joseph and sweet Mary
Could shop in town a bit.

If Magi had been women
Instead of being men,
I'm sure that we'd have peace on earth
And not the mess we're in.

Yes, if Magi had been women
Instead of being guys,
When they had come to Jesus,
They'd been a lot more wise!

-Skin-

Of all the things God's given us,
A million gifts and more,
There's something very special
We should be thankful for.

Can you imagine just how bad
The shape we'd all be in?
How horrible would be our fate
If none of us had skin!

Oh, it is true there'd be no zits
To make teenagers fret,
And racism could not exist;
Yes, that is so but yet

Just what would keep our inners in,
And all the had things out?
Yes, we would all the formless blobs
And have to ooze about.

At Christmas time especially,
We see what skin is worth;
For in it God once robed Himself
When He appeared on earth.

To see Him in a form like us
Upon a manger bed,
To see Him on a rugged cross
Where we should be instead.

Yes, God has given us so much,
A million gifts and more;
But God with skin on is a gift
We should be thankful for!

-Undone-

God has created by His grace
For us on earth a lovely place;
But though He blesses everyone,
There are some things He left undone!

Unbridged God left the rivers wide
For us who seek the other side;
Untrailed He left the deepest wood
And building roads to us who should.

God left the oil in the ground
So that by us it could be found
To put to use by you and me
The power of His energy.

Unbuilt God left the farms and towns,
Unwritten all the music sounds;
He left undone the poetry
To be expressed by you and me.

God left us here a work undone
To be empowered by His Son
So that in love together we
Might all become what we should be.

He could have done it all for man,
But then we would not understand
How unfulfilled our lives would be
If it were done for you and me.

Almighty surely is our King
Who has the power o'er everything;
Yes, there is nothing God can't do

If it were best for me and you.

But let us hear the Lord's decree
That He reveals to you and me,
But the responsibility
To do the work is yours and mine;
The will to do it we must find.

And if we do what e'er God asks,
How blessed then will be each task;
Yes, when we meet our setting sun,
May there be ne'er a task undone!

Made in the USA
Las Vegas, NV
20 December 2021